D0459123

Animals in Order

Ann O. Squire

Anteaters, Sloths, and Armadillos

Franklin Watts - A Division of Grolier Publishing
New York • London • Hong Kong • Sydney • Danbury, Connecticut

For Emma and Evan

Photographs ©: Animals Animals: 39 top (Miriam Agron), 29 (Henry Ausloos), 15 (John Chellman), 5 bottom left (M. Fogden), 35 (Paul Freed), 41 top (Freed Whitehead); BBC Natural History Unit: 7, 33, 42 (Jeff Foott); Michael & Patricia Fogden: 6 right, 17, 19, 21, 23, 39 bottom, 40; Norbert Wu Photography: 8, 38; Peter Arnold Inc.: 5 top right (Luiz C. Marigo); Photo Researchers: 1 (Gregory G. Dimijian), 5 top left (Francois Gohier), 27 (Bud Lehnhausen), 37 (Tom McHugh), 25 (Jany Sauvanet), 31 (M. Wendler/Okapia); Tony Stone Images: 5 bottom right (Norbert Wu); Visuals Unlimited: 41 bottom (Ken Lucas), 6 left (Joe McDonald), cover (William J. Weber).

Illustrations by Jose Gonzales and Steve Savage

Visit Franklin Watts on the Internet at:
http://publishing.grolier.com

Library of Congress Cataloging-in-Publication Data

Squire, Ann O.
Anteaters, sloths, and armadillos / Ann O. Squire
p. cm. — (Animals in order)
Includes bibliographical references and index.
Summary: Discusses the order of the animal kingdom known as xenarthra and describes twelve different species, including the giant anteater, three-toed sloth, hairy armadillo, and pichi.
ISBN 0-531-11515-1 (lib. bdg.) 0-531-15942-6 (pbk.)
1. Xenarthra—Juvenile literature. [1. Armadillos. 2. Anteaters. 3. Sloths] I. Title.
II. Series.
QL737.E2S54 1999
599.3'1—dc21
98-11773
CIP
AC

Printed in the United States of America.
4 5 6 7 8 9 10 R 08 07 06 05 04 03

Contents

Are These Animals Related?

What do you think of when you hear the word "anteater"? How about "sloth" or "armadillo"? You probably think of strange-looking animals that live in far-off places. You may not even be able to picture these animals in your mind. Maybe you've seen them in cartoons or in videos shown at school, but you've probably never seen one in real life.

The pictures on the next page show a pygmy anteater, a three-toed sloth, a giant anteater, and a three-banded armadillo. Can you guess which is which? Believe it or not, all four of these animals are very closely related.

1
2
3
4

Traits of an Xenarthran

Give up? Number 1 is a giant anteater, number 2 is a three-banded armadillo, number 3 is a pygmy anteater, and number 4 is a three-toed sloth. Anteaters, sloths, and armadillos look and act very differently from one another. A giant anteater spends most of its time shuffling along the ground. From time to time, it stops, probes into the dirt with its hard claws, and darts its long tongue into the ground

A giant anteater

A three-toed sloth

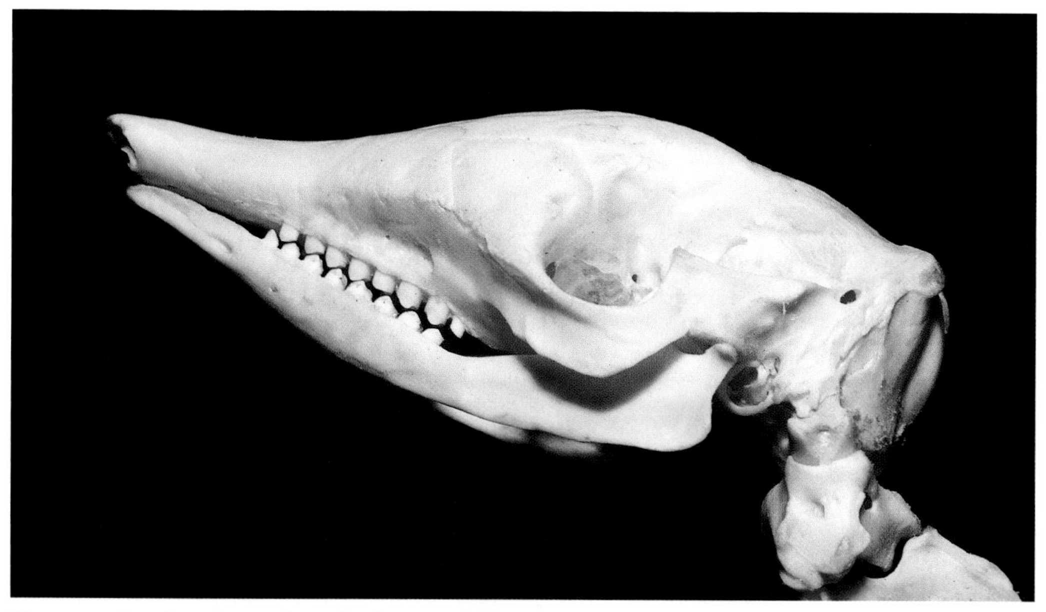

The teeth of a three-banded armadillo are easy to see in this skull.

in search of a hidden ant nest. A three-toed sloth, on the other hand, spends most of its time feasting on leaves as it hangs from tree limbs.

You might find it hard to believe, but these very different animals all belong to the same group, or *order*, of animals. Some scientists call this order edentata, which means "without teeth." However, only anteaters are completely toothless. Sloths and armadillos do have some small teeth, which they use to chew leaves or crunch insects.

Since all these animals aren't toothless, scientists began to look for something else that they have in common. After studying many animals and their skeletons, they found two special features that prove beyond a shadow of a doubt that anteaters, sloths, and armadillos are very closely related.

They all have an unusual connection between the bones in their spine. In most *mammals*, including people, the *vertebrae* that make up the spine are connected by a single pair of *joints*. (A joint is the place where two bones meet.) But in sloths, anteaters, and armadillos, some of the vertebrae are connected by three pairs of joints. This odd arrangement is not found in any other group of mammals on Earth.

The second trait that sloths, anteaters, and armadillos have in common was just as tricky to spot. Their *pelvic bones* are not like

This armadillo is looking for insects in a rotten log.

those of most other animals. Instead of being separate, the bones of the pelvis are fused together, creating a hard, bony "girdle" much like that seen in birds.

Because the traits that set sloths, armadillos, and anteaters apart from other animals are related to their bones and joints, rather than their teeth, scientists decided to rename the group. Today, most scientists say that anteaters, sloths, and armadillos belong to the xenarthran order. They use this name because "xeno-" is the Greek word for "strange" and "arthron" is the Greek word for "joint."

You may wonder how animals that are so closely related can look so different. It is because the common ancestor of anteaters, sloths, and armadillos lived more than 65 million years ago. Since that time, all three animals have changed to adapt to their environments. Today they live in different places and eat different kinds of food.

The Order of Living Things

A tiger has more in common with a house cat than with a daisy. A true bug is more like a butterfly than a jellyfish. Scientists arrange living things into groups based on how they look and how they act. A tiger and a house cat belong to the same group, but a daisy belongs to a different group.

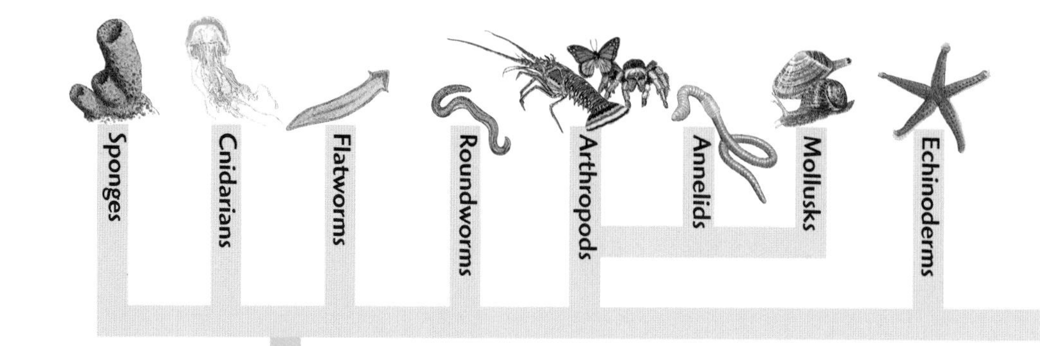

All living things can be placed in one of five groups called *kingdoms*: the plant kingdom, the animal kingdom, the fungus kingdom, the moneran kingdom, or the protist kingdom. You can probably name many of the creatures in the plant and animal kingdoms. The fungus kingdom includes mushrooms, yeasts, and molds. The moneran and protist kingdoms contain thousands of living things that are too small to see without a microscope.

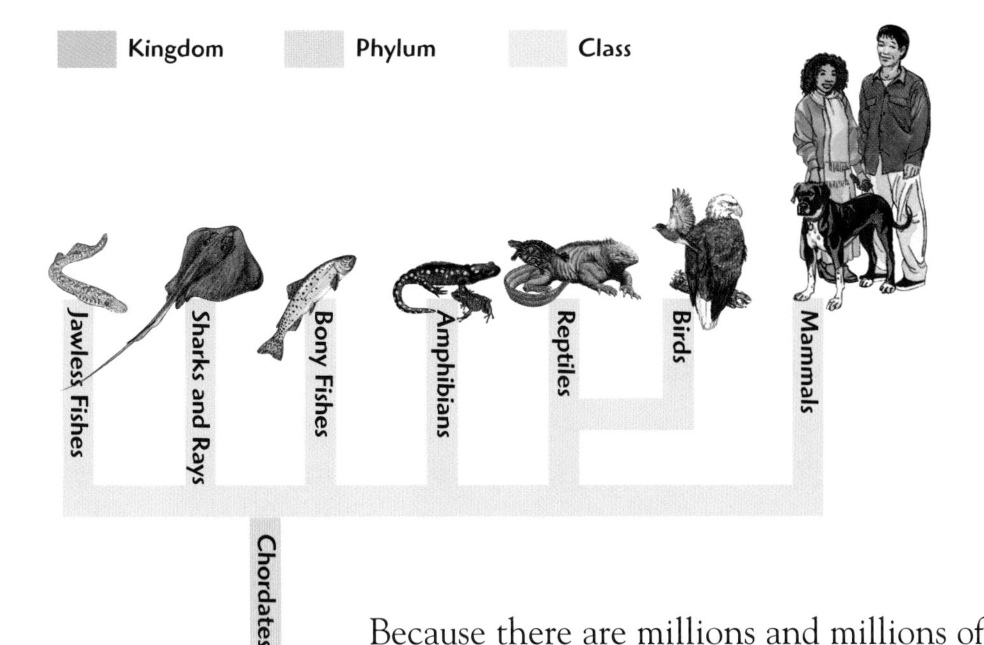

Because there are millions and millions of living things on Earth, some of the members of one kingdom may not seem all that similar. The animal kingdom includes creatures as different as tarantulas and trout, jellyfish and jaguars, salamanders and sparrows, elephants and earthworms.

To show that an elephant is more like a jaguar than an earthworm, scientists further separate the creatures in each kingdom into more specific groups. The animal kingdom can be divided into nine *phyla*. Humans belong to the chordate phylum. Almost all chordates have a backbone.

Each phylum can be subdivided into many *classes*. Humans, mice, and elephants all belong to the mammal class. Each class can be further divided into orders; orders into *families*, families into *genera*, and genera into *species*. All the members of a species are very similar.

How Xenarthrans Fit In

You can probably guess that the xenarthrans—sloths, armadillos, and anteaters—are all members of the animal kingdom. They have much more in common with snakes and sparrows than with maple trees and morning glories.

Xenarthrans belong to the chordate phylum. Almost all chordates have a backbone and a skeleton. Can you think of other chordates? Examples include elephants, mice, snakes, birds, fish, and whales.

The chordate phylum can be divided into a number of classes. Xenarthrans belong to the mammal class. Elephants, humans, dogs, and cats are all mammals.

There are seventeen different orders of mammals. The xenarthrans make up one of these orders. As you learned earlier, anteaters, sloths, and armadillos are grouped together because their skeletons are different from those of other mammals.

The xenarthrans can be divided into several different families and genera. Each genus contains one or more species. You will learn more about twelve species of xenarthrans in this book.

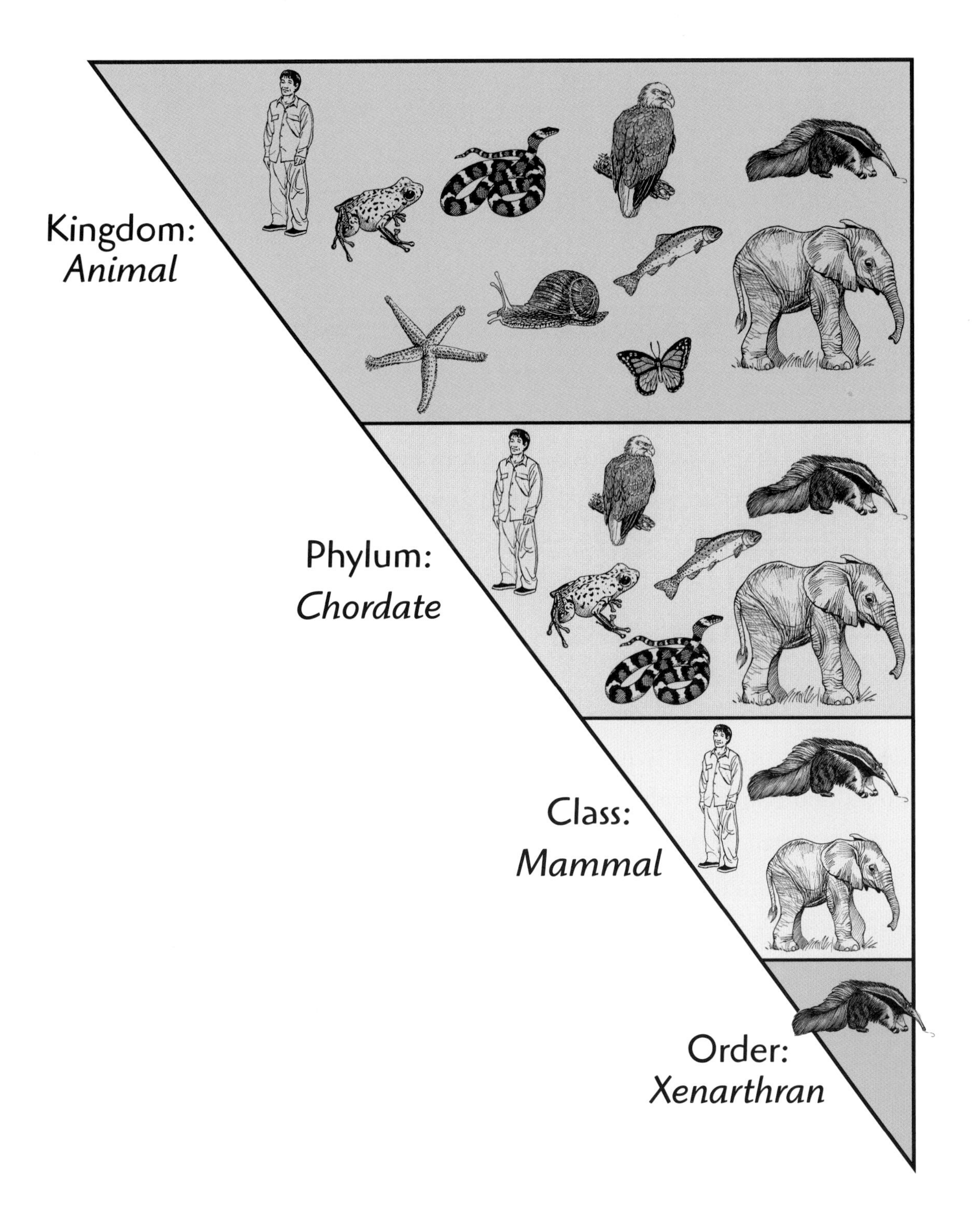

Kingdom:
Animal
Phylum:
Chordate
Class:
Mammal
Order:
Xenarthran

Giant Anteaters

FAMILY: Myrmecophagidae
COMMON NAME: Giant anteater
GENUS AND SPECIES: *Myrmecophaga tridactyla*
SIZE: 5 to 7 feet (150 to 210 cm); 66 to 77 pounds (30 to 35 kg)

Measuring up to 7 feet (2.1 m) long from the tip of its elongated snout to the end of its tasseled tail, this anteater is truly a giant. Of the four anteater species, it is the only one that is regularly active during the day. In the wild, the giant anteater leaves its cozy bed—a shallow trench protected by trees—at mid-morning and spends the day searching for food.

If you could see the dry, grassy plains of South America where many giant anteaters live, you might wonder where this big, lumbering animal could possibly find a meal. The answer is—underground.

Nose to the earth, the anteater moves slowly through the brush. The giant animal relies on its keen sense of smell to find ant or termite nests. Then it uses the 6-inch (15-cm)-long, razor-sharp claws on its front paws to reach the underground nest. After enlarging the hole with its snout, the anteater sticks its long, wet tongue into the nest and snares a mouthful of wriggling insects.

This animal's 22-inch (56-cm) tongue makes it a very efficient *predator*. It's a good thing, since the average giant anteater needs to eat about 35,000 insects every day.

Tamanduas

FAMILY: Myrmecophagidae
COMMON EXAMPLE: Northern tamandua
GENUS AND SPECIES: *Tamandua mexicana*
SIZE: 3 to 5 feet (90 to 150 cm); 8 to 13 pounds (3.5 to 6 kg)

The tamandua, which is also called the lesser anteater or the collared anteater, spends very little time on the ground. This raccoon-sized animal prefers to sleep and hunt in the treetops. It uses its *prehensile tail* to swing from branch to branch.

During the day, the tamandua likes to sleep in hollow trees. When darkness falls, it wakes up and begins a night-long feast on ants and termites. As it prowls through the treetops, the tamandua relies on its ultra-sensitive nose to help it find tasty insects. A tamandua may eat as many as 9,000 ants in a single evening.

If it has trouble finding ants and termites, it will eat bees, honey, or small fruits. Eating fruit must be quite a challenge for an animal with a mouth the diameter of a pencil!

Tamanduas

FAMILY: Myrmecophagidae
COMMON EXAMPLE: Southern tamandua
GENUS AND SPECIES: *Tamandua tetradactyla*
SIZE: 3 to 5 feet (90 to 150 cm); 8 to 13 pounds (3.5 to 6 kg)

The southern tamandua lives in the more southern parts of South America. While the northern tamandua has a "vest" of black fur, the fur of the southern tamandua is just one color. It may be blonde, tan, or brown.

Except during the mating season, the tamandua lives and hunts by itself. If it encounters another animal, the tamandua communicates by hissing or by releasing a powerful, skunk-like odor. Because of its smell, South American natives have named the tamandua "stinker of the forest."

If a tamandua's smell isn't enough to drive another animal away, it doesn't hesitate to fight. If attacked on the ground, the tamandua leans against a tree or rock and wraps its powerful arms around its opponent. If the attack occurs when the tamandua is in a tree, this little animal bares its claws and stretches out its arms until the attacker is within reach. The tamandua's long, strong arms and sharp claws are powerful and effective weapons.

Pygmy Anteaters

FAMILY: Myrmecophagidae
COMMON NAME: Pygmy anteater
GENUS AND SPECIES: *Cyclopes didactylus*
SIZE: 10 to 20 inches (25 to 50 cm); 10 to 17 ounces (280 to 480 grams)

The pygmy anteater, also known as the silky anteater, is the smallest anteater in the world. It is about the same size as a squirrel.

This anteater spends almost all its time in the trees. Like the tamandua, it moves among the branches with the help of its long, grasping tail. Because the pygmy anteater lives high in the trees and is only active at night, scientists don't know much about its behavior.

Like other anteaters, the pygmy anteater eats ants, which it finds on the leaves and branches of trees. Its mouth is large in comparison to the mouths of other anteaters. This allows it to eat a wide variety of foods. Beetles and fruit are regular parts of its diet. While other anteaters rely on their long, sticky tongues to capture food, the pygmy anteater often uses a saliva-covered paw to help push bees and other insects into its mouth.

The pygmy anteater is found throughout tropical forests, but its favorite home seems to be the kapok tree. This may be because the kapok produces soft, fluffy seed pods that look a lot like pygmy anteaters! They are so much alike that if you placed a freshly opened kapok pod next to a pygmy anteater, it would be hard to tell the dif-

ference. What good does this do the anteater? Looking like a seed pod helps the little anteater escape the sharp eyes of owls, eagles, or hawks on the prowl for dinner.

Two-toed Sloths

FAMILY: Choloepidae
COMMON NAME: Two-toed sloth
GENUS AND SPECIES: *Choloepus didactylus*
SIZE: 2 to 3 feet (60 to 90 cm); 9 to 18 pounds (4 to 8 kg)

Like other sloths, the two-toed sloth is best known for its sl-o-o-o-w-w-w lifestyle. A typical two-toed sloth spends most of its day resting—suspended upside down from a tree branch.

For about 7 hours each night, the sloth moves slowly through the treetops munching leaves. Everything about this sloth is slow, even its digestion. A meal of leaves may stay in the sloth's stomach for more than a month before it is completely digested. About once a week, the sloth leaves its treetop home and descends to the ground to pass waste products. Then the sloth climbs back up the tree and resumes its quiet life until the next time it needs to relieve itself.

The female sloth gives birth the same way she does almost everything else—hanging upside down. A newborn sloth, which is about 10 inches (25 cm) long, clings to its mother's fur. It blends in so well that it is barely noticeable. A young sloth is carried by its mother for up to 9 months. During that time, it eats whatever leaves it can reach. By feeding on the same leaves as its mother, the young sloth "inherits" a taste for particular kinds of leaves. As a result, different sloths of the same species have very different leaf preferences.

Three-toed Sloths

FAMILY: Bradypodidae
COMMON EXAMPLE: Pale-throated three-toed sloth
GENUS AND SPECIES: *Bradypus tridactylus*
SIZE: 1.5 to 2 feet (45 to 60 cm); 7 to 11 pounds (3 to 5 kg)

Three-toed sloths and their two-toed relatives eat the same foods and live in the same South American tropical forests. In most ways, they are very similar. Neither type of sloth is what you'd call active, so it's surprising that more sloths don't fall victim to snakes, eagles, or other predators. Many are protected by greenish *algae* (the same algae that grows on ponds) that covers their fur. The algae doesn't seem to bother the sloth at all. In fact, the hairs that make up the sloth's fur have special grooves that provide a good place for the algae to grow.

How does the algae protect the sloth? The green color of the algae makes the sloth hard to spot as it hangs in its leafy treetop. The sloth may also get a quick snack by licking the algae off its own body.

Three-toed Sloths

FAMILY: Bradypodidae
COMMON EXAMPLE: Brown-throated three-toed sloth
GENUS AND SPECIES: *Bradypus variegatus*
SIZE: 1.5 to 2 feet (45 to 60 cm); 7 to 11 pounds (3 to 5 kg)

Unlike other mammals, sloths (both the three-toed and two-toed varieties) have a very low body temperature. While a healthy human has a body temperature of about 98.6 degrees Fahrenheit (37° Celsius), a sloth's body temperature is usually between 86 and 93°F (30 and 34°C).

A sloth's temperature changes with the air temperature. They are cooler at night, during rainy weather, and when they are not active. This kind of variable body temperature is unusual for mammals. In fact, it's more typical of *reptiles*, such as snakes, lizards, and turtles. Scientists think that the slow-moving sloth lowers its body temperature to conserve as much energy as possible.

In the wild, many sloth species are threatened by *habitat* destruction. The tropical forests of South America where three-toed sloths live are rapidly being cut down to produce lumber and charcoal, and to make way for farms and cattle ranches. Unless we take steps to save them, these quiet, gentle creatures may soon be just a memory.

Nine-banded Armadillos

FAMILY: Dasypodidae
COMMON NAME: Nine-banded armadillo
GENUS AND SPECIES: *Dasypus novemcinctus*
SIZE: 2 to 3.5 feet (60 to 105 cm); 6 to 14 pounds (2.7 to 6.4 kg)

A nine-banded armadillo presses its long snout to the ground, snuffling and grunting as it roots through the underbrush. Because it hunts mostly at night, this armadillo depends on its keen sense of smell to help it find insects, worms, and small snakes. The nine-banded armadillo's sense of smell is so good that it can detect *prey* that is 8 inches (20 cm) underground.

Once it has found something to eat, the armadillo digs down until it uncovers its victim. To keep the animal's scent, the armadillo presses its nose to the ground and holds its breath. That way it doesn't inhale dust or dirt. A series of air passages in the nine-banded armadillo's body allows it to hold its breath for up to 6 minutes.

These air passages also come in handy when an armadillo wants to cross streams or small rivers. All it has to do is hold its breath and walk underwater. Or, if the armadillo chooses, it can swim instead. By swallowing enough air to inflate its stomach and intestines, the nine-banded armadillo can float on top of the water. Then it does a simple dog-paddle across the river.

The nine-banded armadillo is the most common kind of armadillo. It is also the only one that lives in some parts of North America. In Brazil, nine-banded armadillos are hunted for their meat, but in the United States their worst enemy is highway traffic.

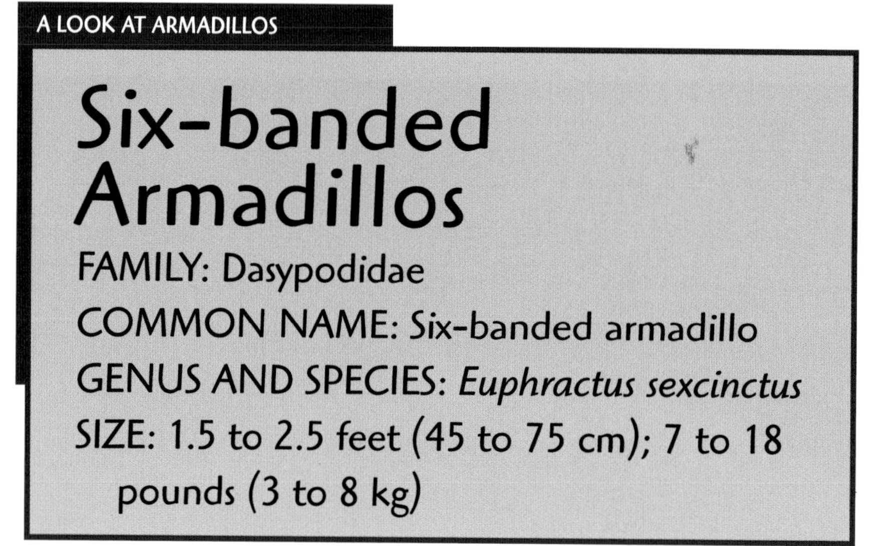

Six-banded Armadillos

FAMILY: Dasypodidae
COMMON NAME: Six-banded armadillo
GENUS AND SPECIES: *Euphractus sexcinctus*
SIZE: 1.5 to 2.5 feet (45 to 75 cm); 7 to 18 pounds (3 to 8 kg)

This six-banded armadillo's flat, pointed head and long tail are covered with armored plates. Although these plates offer some protection, they are not impenetrable. This armadillo is named for the six flexible bands covering its back. However, because it is yellowish-brown, some people call it the yellow armadillo.

If you look closely, you can see tiny holes in a few of the armored plates at the base of the armadillo's tail. What are the holes for? Some scientists believe the scent glands that produce this animal's distinctive odor are located in this area, and that the holes serve as "vents" when the scent is released.

Like other armadillos, this one is a great digger, and continually uncovers new passageways in search of insects. It also sleeps in a den that it digs itself. In fact, the six-banded armadillo digs so many holes that it sometimes creates unstable ground that can be hazardous to other animals. For example, grazing horses have been injured when they accidentally stumbled into an armadillo's grass-covered *burrow*.

Unlike many other armadillos, the six-banded armadillo is active during the day, and can be seen foraging for food even in bright daylight.

Hairy Armadillos

FAMILY: Dasypodidae
COMMON NAME: Hairy armadillo
GENUS AND SPECIES: *Chaetophractus villosus*
SIZE: 1.5 to 2 feet (45 to 60 cm); 4 to 5 pounds (1.8 to 2.3 kg)

Hairy armadillos are a lot hairier than other armadillos. Their bellies and legs are covered with white or light brown hairs. They even have hairs growing between the scales that make up their body armor.

Hairy armadillos usually live in hot, dry desert areas, and escape the heat by tunneling deep into sand dunes. In the summer, they avoid the heat by hunting for food at night. In the winter, when air temperatures are cooler, they often hunt above ground during the day.

Although hairy armadillos eat mostly insects and plants, they sometimes feed on lizards, rodents, and small snakes. One hairy armadillo was seen killing a snake by jumping on it and cutting it in half with the sharp edge of its armor!

When being chased by a predator, the hairy armadillo first tries to escape into its burrow, often snarling and growling in an attempt to discourage its enemy. If its burrow is too far away, the armadillo tries to dig itself a new hole in the ground. As a last resort, the hairy armadillo lies down and pulls in its feet so that the edges of

its coat of armor touch the ground. Imagine how frustrated a hungry hawk or coyote feels when its frightened prey is suddenly transformed into a smooth, hard, impenetrable shell!

Three-banded Armadillos

FAMILY: Dasypodidae
COMMON NAME: Three-banded armadillo
GENUS AND SPECIES: *Tolypeutes matacus*
SIZE: 1.5 to 2 feet (45 to 60 cm); 3 to 4 pounds (1.4 to 1.8 kg)

Many people believe that armadillos are best known for their ability to roll up into a tight ball when threatened. However, only the three-banded armadillo can protect itself in this way.

When it senses danger, the three-banded armadillo tries to run away. If it cannot outrun its enemy, this little animal pulls its feet in and snaps its shoulder and hip shields together to form a tight, round ball. Even the strongest dogs, wolves, and coyotes usually cannot pry open this hard sphere.

The armadillo's tough armor does more than just protect it from enemies. It also shelters the armadillo from the weather. Air trapped underneath the thick shell surrounds the armadillo's body and insulates it—almost like a down coat.

Like other armadillos, the three-banded armadillo eats mostly ants and termites. But these armadillos do not dig their own burrows. They sleep in abandoned anteater burrows instead. In a pinch, they may even sleep under bushes.

Pichi

FAMILY: Dasypodidae
COMMON NAME: Pichi
GENUS AND SPECIES: *Zaedyus pichiy*
SIZE: 14 to 15 inches (36 to 38 cm); 2 to 4 pounds (0.9 to 1.8 kg)

The pichi is a quiet creature that prefers to live alone. Because coarse, bristly hair covers its belly and the edges of the armored plates on its back, this animal is sometimes called the bristled armadillo.

The pichi looks a lot like a six-banded armadillo, but is smaller. As a result, scientists once thought that the two armadillos were closely related. In reality, however, pichis are much more closely related to hairy armadillos.

The pichi is found in the grasslands of Argentina and Chile, where it digs shallow holes in the sandy soil. When confronted by an enemy, the pichi pulls in its feet so that the edges of its armored shell touch the ground. The pichi may also anchor itself into its burrow by wedging the jagged edges of its armored plates into the surrounding dirt. When a pichi is in this position, all its predators see is a smooth, hard shell.

Pichis are still very common in their natural habitat, and are often hunted in South America. Sometimes people even keep them as house pets.

Many armadillo species cope with the cold by lowering their body temperature or hunting for food during the day. The pichi does both of these things, but it has another cold weather strategy too. It is the only armadillo that can escape winter altogether by simply sleeping through it. The pichi *hibernates*.

Fun Facts About Anteaters, Sloths, and Armadillos

- The difference between two-toed sloths and three-toed sloths is not the number of toes they have, but the number of fingers! While all sloths have three toes on each hind foot, two-"toed" sloths have two fingers on each hand and three-"toed" sloths have three fingers on each hand.

- *Vermilingua*, the scientific name for anteaters, means "worm-tongued." All four species of anteaters use their long, sticky wormlike tongues to probe for food in underground ant and termite nests.
- Both two- and three-toed sloths spend nearly their entire lives upside down. They eat, mate, give birth, and sleep while hanging from tree limbs.

- Although they seem calm and gentle, sloths can and do defend themselves. Their chief weapons are their teeth and their sharp, hooked claws, both of which can inflict serious wounds on an animal foolish enough to attack them.

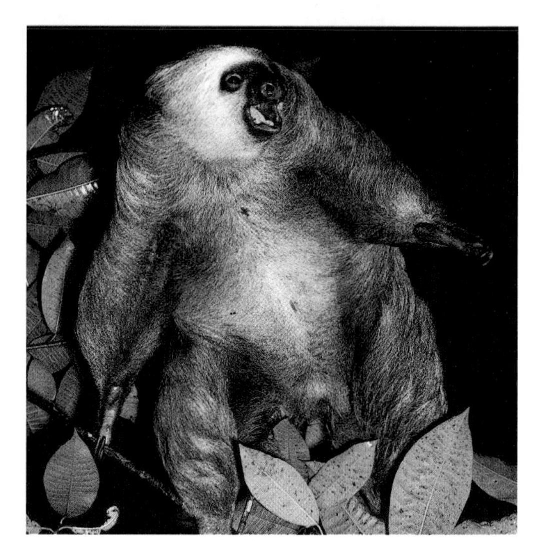

- All sloths spend most of their lives in trees, coming down to the ground as seldom as possible. Although they are agile climbers, sloths cannot walk. They must move around on the ground by dragging themselves along with their claws. This makes them easy prey for jaguars, ocelots, and other ground-dwelling predators.

- Although they look prehistoric, armadillos are the most widespread of all the xenarthrans. They are found throughout South and Central America and in parts of North America as well. One species, the nine-banded armadillo, lives throughout the southeastern United States, and has been seen as far north as Missouri and Colorado.
- Because armadillos have many unusual traits, they are popular subjects for scientific experiments. For example, they are the only animals known to develop leprosy, a serious human disease. Studying armadillos has helped scientists learn how to treat and prevent this disease in humans.

- Nine-banded armadillos have their babies in the spring, and almost always produce identical quadruplets. Closely related armadillo species are also known for multiple births: the Brazilian lesser long-nosed armadillo, for example, gives birth to four, eight, or even twelve identical babies.

Words to Know

algae—tiny living things that live in watery habitats.

burrow—an animal shelter dug in the ground.

class—a group of creatures within a phylum that share certain characteristics.

family—a group of creatures within an order that share certain characteristics.

genus (plural **genera**)—a group of creatures within a family that share certain characteristics.

habitat—the environment where a plant or animal lives and grows.

hibernate—to spend the winter in a deep sleep, with slowed heart rate and breathing.

joint—the area where two bones come together.

kingdom—one of the five divisions into which all living things are placed: the animal kingdom, the plant kingdom, the fungus kingdom, the moneran kingdom, and the protist kingdom.

mammal—an animal that has a backbone and feeds its young with mother's milk.

order—a group of organisms within a class that share certain characteristics.

pelvic bone—one of the bones that form the hips of many animals.

phylum (plural **phyla**)—a group of creatures within a kingdom that share certain characteristics.

predator—an animal that catches and feeds on other animals.

prehensile tail—a tail that can be used for grabbing and grasping.

prey—an animal hunted for food by another animal (a predator).

reptile—a group of animals that are covered with scales and lay eggs on land. Examples include snakes, turtles, crocodiles, and lizards.

species—a group of organisms within a genus that share certain characteristics. Members of a species can mate and produce young.

vertebra (plural **vertebrae**)—one of the bony segments that makes up the spine (backbone) of many animals.

Learning More

Books

Adelman, Elizabeth Fagan and Jan Wills. *Rand McNally Children's Atlas of World Wildlife*. New York: Rand McNally, 1990.

Grzimek, Bernhard. *Grzimek's Animal Life Encyclopedia*. New York: McGraw-Hill, 1990.

Hartman, Jane. *Armadillos, Anteaters and Sloths: How They Live*. New York: Holiday House, 1980.

Jenike, David and Mark. *A Walk Though a Rainforest*. New York: Franklin Watts, 1994.

Landau, Elaine. *Tropical Rainforests Around the World*. New York: Franklin Watts, 1990.

Macdonald, David. *The Encyclopedia of Mammals*. New York: Facts on File, 1984.

Maynard, Catlin and Thane Maynard. *Rain Forests and Reefs*. Danbury, CT: Franklin Watts, 1996.

Robinson, Fay. *The Upside-Down Sloth*. Danbury, CT: Children's Press, 1993.

Web Sites

This site has some basic information about anteaters and compares them to an unrelated Australian animal called the spiny anteater. Its address is:

http://edx1.educ.monash.edu.au/~juanda/vcm/behzad.htm.

This site lists some interesting facts about anteaters as well as important information about their habitat, lifestyle, and physical features. It can be reached at:
http://www.meerkat.org/mammals/ganteat.htm.

This site has general information about two-toed sloths and three-toed sloths as well as a list of places where you can visit sloths and links to several other related sites, some of which include photos. It can be reached at:
http://www.geocities.com/Hollywood/Set/1478/sloth.html.

This is a great site. *Armadillos Online*! offers a tremendous variety of information about armadillos and scientific research being done to learn even more about them. The site includes photos and links to other sites that discuss armadillos. Its address is:
http://www.msu.edu/user/nixonjos/index.htm/.

Index

About the Author

Ann O. Squire, who holds a Ph.D. in animal behavior, has studied a variety of animals, including rats and electric fish. She is the author of several other books on animal behavior, including *101 Questions and Answers About Backyard Wildlife* and *Understanding Man's Best Friend: Why Dogs Look and Act the Way They Do*. Dr. Squire lives with her family in Pelham, New York.